THE ART
and SCIENCE
of PICKING
WINNING
HORSES

T0119272

THE ART
and SCIENCE
of PICKING
WINNING
HORSES

JAMES HILLIS

GBC PRESS
P. O. Box 98115
Las Vegas, NV 89193
www.gamblersbookclub.com

GBC Press books are published by Gambler's Books Club in Las Vegas, Nevada. Since 1964, the legendary GBC has been the reigning authority on gambling publications and the only dedicated gambling bookstore anywhere.

Copyright © 2011 by Gamblers Book Club
All Rights Reserved

Library of Congress Catalog Number: 2011925830
ISBN 10: 1-58042-281-0   ISBN 13: 978-1-58042-281-9
GBC Press is an imprint of Cardoza Publishing

GBC PRESS

c/o Cardoza Publishing
P.O. Box 98115, Las Vegas, NV 89193
Toll-Free Phone (800)522-1777
email: info@gamblersbookclub.com
www.gamblersbookclub.com

James Hillis is a longtime horseracing handicapper who has compiled the lifetime of his winning secrets into *The Art and Science of Picking Winning Horses.*

TABLE OF CONTENTS

1 INTRODUCTION

Handicapping is a science and an art. In this book, I'm going to show you how to progress from pure betting and depending upon chance or hunches, to taking calculated risks, which entails knowledge and judgment; in other words, how to bet like a winner!

I'll show you how to analyze the real factors that influence a race and eliminate horses that have little chance of winning—narrowing the short list of winners and immediately increasing your chances of cashing tickets. You'll learn which races are difficult to predict and should be avoided, and likewise, the races that can best be handicapped and where the profit can be found. I've included more than 50 key factors for beating the horses and the key secrets I have used and track-tested for decades.

This work is arranged as a sort of textbook. The several aspects of handicapping are presented in an orderly and progressively instructive fashion, with exercises to practice handicapping. My purpose is to make you familiar with nearly all the elements that should enter into professional selection. I do not mean that you should perpetually apply these exercises in each and every race, but I do suggest that to correctly learn selection, you should spend sufficient time on them to become aware of the relative importance of each element.

I also suggest effective shortcuts, but no matter what shortcut you end up using, you will need to know all the basic principles. Without such knowledge, you will not recognize the danger that always lurks in an abbreviated formula for choosing winning prospects. Moreover, there will be many races in which a shortcut will show no clear-cut prospect. Sometimes, the abbreviated method will not turn up a good prospect in a whole afternoon. On such occasions, the longer methods, though cumbersome and time-consuming, are your only alternative to passing up the race or the day. Therefore, be patient and do the exercises suggested.

This book gives you the basic information and advice you need to make horseracing the enjoyable and economical hobby it can and should be. It does not presume to do your thinking for you, but it does point out the lines along which your thinking must run—and in betting, that is most important. This book aims to turn you away from pure gambling on the horses and into taking calculated risks.

That is the path to winning money at horseracing!

2 HANDICAPPING: A SMART BET OR A GAMBLE?

Probably most plays at the track are the result of tips, or perhaps faith in a jockey, owner or trainer. The tips come from the newspaper selectors, the "dope sheets" sold near or at the track, the person next to you, someone who knows the jockey, and so on. It amounts to gambling that the other fellow knows what he is doing.

If you must follow a tipster, you are usually safest with the public professional handicappers whose selections appear in the newspapers, the racing form, or the "dope sheets." Neither taking their tips nor making longshot bets will give you a consistent profit. This is statistically certain. The best public handicappers may average three wins out of ten selections. While that in itself could be enough to show a profit, in the case of public handicappers, it does not. So many follow their suggestions that the odds are usually depressed too low on the three winners to offset the losses on the seven.

It may well be that the expensive private professionals have a better record with their selections, but I doubt that over the long run, one can make anything even with them. It seems to me that if the private selector had any real confidence in his own choices, he would do better financially to go to the races and bet on those choices!

If one does not want to learn the horses himself and still prefers to follow the consensus of the "dopesters," he might do all right if he passed up those races in which the selection went to post at less than certain odds, say two to one. But all of this is by the way. This book is for those bettors who are interested in gaining the knowledge necessary for their own handicapping. Your own handicapping is the only kind that will consistently pay off. The very fact that we independent bettors back our studies with a cash investment indicates that we have more faith in our choices than the public handicapper has in his.

Since racing deals with interested human beings and trained animals, some forecast must be possible in any race. In fact, the forecasting made by race fans is usually pretty good. This is evident from the fact that 30 to 35 percent of the horses selected by the majority of bettors win the race. It is also clear from the fact that the horse that wins is usually well backed, as evidenced by the odds.

I doubt, however, that the most money in any race derives from the blind or the tip-conscious bettor. Those who use the forms make heavier plays, and the very heavy bettors usually know what they are doing.

GAMBLING OR TAKING A CALCULATED RISK?

He who merely gambles at the track may be very successful in one or another race, or on one or another day, but in the long run he will come off a loser. This is mathematically certain for the simple reason that 15 to 20 percent of every dollar wagered is taken out of the pool before it is distributed among the holders of winning tickets. As a result, the person who depends on chance alone cannot hope to do better than lose 15 to 20 percent of the total amount he bets. Those who depend on chance alone are actually betting against people who know horses and who, therefore, are not gambling. It is this feature that accounts for the terrific losses suffered by hunch bettors.

The difference between gambling and taking a calculated risk is this: The calculated risk in handicapping the horses, just as in any other venture, is taken on the basis of knowledge and judgment. The gambler depends on chance. For a chance player, one race or horse is as good as another. The calculator, on the other hand, may pass up some races or may bet heavier or lighter depending on the degree of his certainty. Even if he finds but two or three races to his liking in an afternoon, he is quite content. Occasionally he may skip the whole card or make nominal bets for fun alone.

In fact, at all tracks you will find quiet, unobserved bettors who are getting great joy out of the events and who, at the same time, are making a very comfortable living by conservative, investment plays. Their secret is the one that this book will teach you.

Neither I nor any other author who writes on this subject will have any noticeable effect on track odds. The horse-playing crowd will go on in the way it always has. Very few will want to be bothered with the study and caution needed for businesslike betting. It is this carefree group that furnishes the money picked up by the quiet, studious hobbyist.

Uninhibited bettors merit our respect. While financing racing, they really enjoy it. For them, a day at the track is well worth the loss they may take. They would spend as much in a nightclub, with no chance of recovering anything and with nothing for their money but a hangover. For them, one good day at the races offsets any chagrin they may have suffered in a previous half dozen unlucky afternoons. It takes all of us to make a world.

Your personal judgment based on your own observation of facts is essential to successful betting. If you are one of those few who have keen powers of observation, the ability to see the whole picture, and good, practical judgment, this book gives you all you need to know for consistent overall success at the track.

KNOWLEDGE OF THE PAST IS ESSENTIAL

To forecast any future event, *knowledge of the past is absolutely indispensable.* In the early days of racing, the general public did not have access to the past performance records of either the humans or the animals on the track. It was the few who kept personal records or who had phenomenal memories who were able to gain an advantage. This has long since changed. Nearly everything about the ability and preparation of a horse is now available to the general public. The only thing the public may not know is what instructions the jockey has received, but even then, the bettor has at his disposal enough facts to tell him when to skip a race. Nothing in the racing profession can long remain an enigma. All the important information is soon exposed.

I'm going to show you how to use that information to your advantage.

3 EVALUATING A RACE AND YOUR BETS

The *Daily Racing Form* contains everything that is essential for you to take a calculated risk. For perfection, we would like to see the manner in which the horses ran their most recent race or two transferred to the performance chart. We would like to see signs for the various kinds of trouble, and for the way in which the winners and other good performers finished; for example, whether the horse won driving, handily, or so on. But you can find this information in another part of the *Daily Racing Form*, or in the back numbers that are reported in detail on the recent events in which the horse was entered.

A comparison of morning odds and post odds is sometimes helpful. Morning odds are given in another part of the *Daily Racing Form*. Selections of public handicappers are also sometimes helpful. Some of these are found in the racing daily, others in the day's newspapers and on he Internet. (Note that the dope sheets sold at the track may not influence the betting sufficiently to be of use.)

This book teaches you to bet smart using only the *Daily Racing Form* (or its equivalent on the Internet). The rest will come in time if you are the perfectionist type. Interpreted correctly, the facts you gather will give you enough winners to more than repay your effort. Of course, this means that you must have a complete understanding of the information, which, in the *Daily Racing Form*, is readily available in each issue.

ESSENTIAL INFO FOR JUDGING HORSES

In a race, the horse is by far the most important consideration. If a horse has not shown that he has it on the ball, no human agency can supplement his deficiencies. But if he does have it on the ball and the competition in a specific race is keen, then the humans associated with him are important. Let's look at that now.

As far as the horse is concerned, there are several essential considerations. His record shows what he can do. Do not judge this ability by what he has done in a workout, but by what has occurred in *actual* competitive races. Many a horse with a brilliant workout fades on the track. Further, what a horse showed he could do last year or the year before is of little or no value today. But if, in the last twelve months or so, he has done about what he is called upon to do today, he may be a prospect for victory.

I say that he *may* be a prospect because on that ground alone, he is not. Like any member of the animal kingdom, including man, a horse must have training right up to the event in which he is to compete. This training, of course, should not be continuous for the whole year. Rest periods are essential. But there is no substitute for competitive racing and workouts just before today's event just as there is no substitute for parallel preparation in the case of a boxer, ballplayer or golfer.

What the horse has done in the past year shows only what he can do. It is what he has been doing in the last month or so that tells us whether or not he actually will do today what he is called upon to accomplish.

ESSENTIAL INFO FOR JUDGING THE HUMAN ELEMENT

None of the humans involved in horseracing—owner, trainers and jockeys—is of any great importance when the horse's record indicates that he is definitely superior to the field in which he is running today. However, if the competition is keen, if it looks as though the winner will make it by less than a length, then the human element can be important. Where just a little more know-how is found in a jockey or trainer, or just a little more sagacity has been observed in an owner, it can pay off in the races of closely matched animals.

The information you need to classify owners, trainers and jockeys appears from time to time in the newspaper or the *Daily Racing Form*, or can readily be found on the Internet. In the case of owners and trainers, you take the total number of race entries during the last year or two and divide into that the number of wins to his credit. The lower the resulting figure, the better the human. With jockeys, take only the total of his mounts this meet or, if this meet is not yet half over, take the total of his mounts last meet and this meet. Into this number, divide the number of his wins. Again, the lower the result, the better the jockey.

In the case of owners and trainers, consider only the six best. Jockeys who have less than one win in twenty races hardly merit rating for our purposes. The top jockey at any meet may average one win in four or fewer mounts; the next group, one in five to eight mounts; the third group, one in nine to twelve rides; and the fourth group, one in thirteen to twenty rides. All other jockeys would fall into a fifth group.

THE IMPORTANCE OF THE JOCKEY

The jockey is the most important human element in a close race, but only when he is aboard a horse that might win with any jockey. Do not bet much money when your confidence is divided between the horse and his rider. It is by no means evident that the actual ability of any given jockey agrees with this system or rating. The so-called better jockeys win more often—not exclusively because they are so much better, but because, having a reputation, their agents are always sure of having a mount and therefore choose the best horse available.

Then, too, when an owner feels that his horse has a better chance, he will often select the best jockey he can get. In fact, a change in jockeys after scratches often indicates a winner. The change need not be drastic: A move from a fifth-class to a fourth-class jockey is enough. A jockey change is, of course, without significance when it has been caused by the incapacitation of the original selection.

Horses ridden by apprentice jockeys are given an apprentice "allowance," say five pounds off on weight. The horse usually needs that and more to compensate for the rider's inexperience. Except where the apprentice is well above average, think twice before backing the mount of an apprentice. The reasoning that chooses the five-pound advantage rather than the experience of the jockey is seldom good. The only time it pays off is where the jockey has shown real talent despite his youth.

The fact that a promising jockey often fades when he loses the "bug" (his apprentice standing) is nothing against the young man. It means merely that he has to take potluck with his mounts. He is no longer singled out by trainers who want both his talent and the weight advantage to be more sure that the horse has everything possible in his favor.

Where horses are front runners going in long races, old-timers in the jockey profession get the best results. It takes long experience rather than native talent for the man on the front horse to conserve his mount's energy without having other animals to gauge it by.

THE BETTOR

Another human element is the bettor. As a rule, we should not despise the judgment of those who place bets in any specific race. Even in a holiday crowd with all its wild bettors, there are usually sufficient solid players to make a noticeable impression on the odds. This little group makes larger bets and just one of them often offsets a couple of hundred $2.00 wagers. That the money crowd is using good judgment, as a rule, is evident from the fact that nearly all races are won by a horse paying under 10 to 1, and much less than half that on the average. It is also evident from the fact that one of the three or four horses going to post at the lowest odds usually ends up first at the wire. Even the favorite will win three to four races out of ten, despite the fact that he often becomes the favorite by excess betting on the part of people who depend on dope sheets.

On most tracks, it is easier to handicap in summer and fall (May to November) than in winter and spring. The mounts will have longer recent records, all of which will have been on fast tracks. The percentage of longshot winners drops. Nevertheless, we should not be guided in our own choices by track odds alone. They should serve only as a check. If the odds on our selection do not look right, we should take another look at our *Daily Racing Form*.

Some confirmed and rather successful players do not bet unless they see a horse they like among the first three on the odds list. As noted above, such players will do better in the summer. Favorites going to post at less than even money are usually a fair investment. But bettors who play only at such odds make very little money—and also have a dull afternoon. The *Daily Racing Form* user who considers the odds merely as signs to strengthen or weaken his conclusions will come away far better off financially.

TAKING CALCULATED RISKS

You cannot always win. While it is neither necessary nor advisable to take a chance on a race, there is always a risk and a calculated risk we must take. Three elements make any race a risk.

1. **The Trouble Facor**
   In the first place, trouble of one kind or another can befall any horse or rider.
2. **The Random Factor**
   Secondly, in a few cases where your horse's past performance recommends him, he just does not deliver.
3. **The Psychlogical Factor**
   The third and most common factor is the psychological element of the bettor. Even the best-informed bettor will have off-days, probably even two or three in a row. That could be fatal to a bettor who seeks to recover his losses by doubling up on subsequent plays—but it is of little consequence if you stick to the 10 percent rule.

I call this third factor "psychological," because as a rule off-days cannot be explained by the field that is running, nor by that indefinite expression you so often hear, "This is not my lucky day." The reason is far more simple and sensible. It lies in the fact that the human mind is not at all times equally keen and objective. Many things can happen that upset a person's powers of observation, analysis and judgment. Distractions from business or family reverses, the presence of someone irritating, preconceived notions in one or another race—these are just examples of the real reasons behind the errors that result in sour bets.

But because you foresee such days occurring, they do not disturb you. As you come to detect the causes of your off-days, you will either avoid the track at those times, or avoid *at the track* what is causing the trouble. Some lad sticking his head over your shoulder each race and asking, "What are you betting on this time?" can upset your applecart.

BETTING ON LONGSHOTS

A rather common bettor's malady is consistent longshot betting, with or without recommending qualities in the selection. Occasionally selecting a longshot is the normal result of good handicapping—but looking for one in every race is a disease!

The consistent longshot player's downfall also is a matter of statistics. If he chooses $9.00 horses, he will find that no consistent player of such horses can break even on any track. In fact, the longer the odds, the less often, even proportionately, does the horse come in. A horse paying $9.00 will win once in about twelve times, whereas one paying $12.00 will win once in eighteen times. So playing longshots just because they are longshots is not even good gambling.

WIN, PLACE OR SHOW?

From the business viewpoint, bets to win are best. In the first place, it is easier to forecast the winner than the horse that will place or show. In fact, those who play place and show select the mount they think *should* win, but bet place or show to be on the safe side.

On the other hand, a horse has twice the chance to place that he has to win and three times the chance to show, but this is usually offset by the odds. In fact, a horse paying 6 to 1 to win, 3 to 1 to place and 2 to 1 to show could be bet any way from the viewpoint of an investment. In reality, however, odds do not come out that way. With rare exceptions, the horses pay considerably less than half to place and much less than a third to show. If you frequently go to the races, you should bet only when you are quite sure your choice is right and you should always bet him to win. If you only occasionally go to the track, you will want to bet on most races. Place or show bets are then quite in order when there is a doubt in your mind.

While you are learning to judge horses by the observations made in this book, it is just as well to make place bets. At first you will have many near misses. During that period, it might also be well to choose from the three or four horses showing the lowest odds.

When an entry is running and both mounts have a good chance of being in the money, a place and show bet can be better than one to win. Also, on rare occasions a mount will pay more to place than win, or nearly as much. These are fine points you will learn by experience.

It may take a couple of months and a dozen visits to the track before you get the knack of spotting the races that are to be played and those which may as well be skipped. You will also have to nurse your sores from some bad plays you just could not resist making despite the uncertainty which, in fact, plagued the race!

WORST AND BEST RACES TO FORECAST

Always remember that in most cases, it is not possible to forecast the winner with any degree of certainty. Such races are played only for fun. If you need to place a couple of bucks on a horse's nose in order to enjoy a race, you might keep some money in another pocket and use it there. When the pocket is empty, replenish it by going without other costly but less enjoyable pleasures. Plays on such races are never business propositions. Even at that, your knowledge of horses will make you fare better than the average bettor in such events.

DIFFICULT RACES TO FORECAST

In general, the races listed in the box are difficult and often impossible to forecast:

DIFFICULT RACES TO FORECAST
1. Two-year-olds
2. Maidens
3. Quarterhorses
4. Races under six furlongs or over a mile and a quarter
5. Races in the mud, on the turf, or at substandard tracks
6. Cheap claimers
7. Races where the steeds are over nine years old
8. Handicaps and other similar events when the purse is large, say $50,000 or more

In some of these cases, the horses are unreliable or have not yet developed a form (two-year-olds, maidens, cheap or old steeds). In others, there is too much room for chance—quarterhorses, mud or turf races, very short or very long races, substandard tracks. In the big purse events, competition is often too keen despite the reliability and excellence of the entrants. Steeplechases, hurdles and harness races are beyond the scope of this book. It is probable that turf and mud races could be forecast if there were more of them. Nevertheless, the ideas found in this book should be a genuine help even in "off races" such as those referred to above.

THE BEST RACES TO BET

As for distance, the most common short race is six furlongs. It is also the best short distance for betting purposes. The most common long race is the mile and one-sixteenth. It is also the safest distance for bettors. The best horse has plenty of time to get down to work and not enough time to overexert himself. All races from six furlongs to a mile and a quarter are good distances for betting.

In the period we are using for our examples, thirteen out of twenty-one races at a mile and one-sixteenth, and eleven out of twenty-one at six furlongs present a good prospect for a bet. Most good bets seem to show up in claiming races, but on the other hand, these are also the most numerous events.

There are, however, certain runs even in the acceptable classes on which you cannot make a good, calculated-risk bet. In a nine-race card, the average is about three relatively safe plays. It is often said that Mondays and Fridays are bad days for bettors. In general, I have not found this to be the case. So far as I can see, one day is as good as another.

BETTING TO WIN

A horse merits a sizeable wager only when his record makes it seem clear that he will win convincingly—in other words, by a length or more. In fact, if you have placed a maximum bet on a horse that wins by a nose, don't pat yourself on the back. Just thank your lucky stars or the jockey! If you were a good handicapper, you would have bet less on him. Exception: Sometimes you have done all right on the handicapping and still win or lose by a nose, but this is usually true only when unforeseeable trouble has beset your horse, or when you chose the mount because of his demonstrated courage in the face of horses just as fast as he is.

Never bet on more than one horse in any race, no matter when the urge comes and no matter how strong it is. Win or lose, stick to your bet and it alone. Some good players take one win and two place tickets on their choice, but no seasoned player will make any kinds of bets on more than one horse.

Whereas a place bet instead of a win bet is reasonable enough where competition is keen or when odds are relatively better on place, a show bet is very seldom indicated. As a rule, one may start his career with place bets and advance to win when he has sharpened his wits. In the long run, despite the loss you will sometimes take by your horse coming in second, the favorable odds on win will readily offset losses. The problem with the show bets arises from the fact that the odds are so low, it often takes several cashable show tickets to recover from one show loss.

Here is another important point in betting to win: While it is true that most horses that go to post at less than even money come in often enough for the consistent player on this type to make a profit, that profit is too small to pay expenses unless you have plenty of money to invest. All in all, a horse that does not pay even money or better does not rate a bet unless he is so far above his competition that the lowest apprentice can bring him in by a couple of lengths or more. There are such horses! But strange as it may seem, there are far more horse just as good that go to post at odds of 2 to 1, and on rare occasions as high as 8 or 9 to 1. So, do not lose any sleep over passing up a race in which the odds on your choice (your "sure shot") are depressed below 5 to 8 ($3.20 for a $2.00 ticket).

This is something that experience at the track will teach you if you are the type with a good eye for business. If you do not have the eye, you will be no more successful at the track than you would be in the stock market or, for that matter, in a junk store!

Now, let us move forward to examine and learn how to determine the winning characteristics of steeds.

5 THE SIGNS OF A WINNING HORSE

I do not profess to give you a system to follow in choosing winners, but rather to bring to your attention the signs in horses that can make them winners on the day they race. There are at least thirty points to look for in a winner and six points that can prevent a good horse from winning. These points are independent of three other considerations: post position, jockey and odds changes. Furthermore, some of the points that are against a horse in a short race may be in his favor in a long one and vice versa. I will explain each point, and indicate seven points that are very significant and quickly observable in the *Daily Racing Form.* Beginners may concern themselves with those seven points only, and gradually absorb the others.

Playing the horses in a proper manner takes work and any notion that one can qualify for it without careful study is strictly unreasonable. As in any other science, we live in an age when the knowledge gained by the experience of many can be collected into organized form and be assimilated with relative ease. But in racing, as in any trade or profession, there is no substitute for concentration and personal experience. I can point out what to look for and how to evaluate what you find, but I cannot push this information into your blood stream. Yet it must be there. It must become a part of you, so much so that you will not have to refer to any notes when you make your selections. Only your personal application, study and perseverance can create in you this mentality.

At first reading, you may get a bit confused, but have patience. Just remember that you are trying to digest conclusions in a few hours that have taken years of patient research to formulate and correlate.

So let what I say sink in. Try to apply what you learn at home first. Do not go to the track until you see the light, until you are able to spot in the race card a couple of horses that actually win convincingly. When you do go to the races, do not be discouraged that so much happening around you tends to confuse your thinking. After a few visits, you will gain your composure. Now let us delve into the characteristics of winners.

WHAT MAKES A HORSE A WINNER?

A convincing winner is one that wins easily, handily, breezing or even driving when he outdistances his competition by a length or more.

The most common characteristic of the convincing winner is overall gain between the first call and the wire. The second most desirable quality in a horse is his ability to gain in the stretch. The third quality is of very great importance in short races. This is the ability to break fast and reach the first call at or near the head of the pack. Such horses are called front runners. In long races this quality alone seems to be rather against a horse than in his favor.

Actually, because of their great importance, these three points about a horse are listed out of their logical order. But these characteristics alone are not effective, by any means. For example, a horse whose record shows that he possesses these traits can trail the field if he has been away from the track for more than thirty days.

With these points out of the way, let us settle down to the signs for a winner and consider them in an orderly fashion. These are the questions we want answered:

1. Has the horse done, or at least come near doing, what he is asked to do today?
2. Has the horse been given a recent opportunity to fit himself for a repeat of what he has done before?
3. Does the horse's record in these recent outings show that he will do today what he has done before, or even better?
4. If his recent record is not as commendable as that of some of his running mates, is the horse getting a break from his owner or the track stewards that will offset this poor recent showing?

By examining the characteristics of potential winners, we will be able to answer all of these questions.

CHARACTERISTICS OF POTENTIAL WINNING HORSES

1. A HORSE'S CLASS OR POTENTIAL

The only evidence we have as to what a horse can do is the record of what he has done. Since the age of the horse and his trainers change a horse's ability, we must judge from the last year or so. There are three things in the *Daily Racing Form* that will tell us at a glance what a horse can do.

What are his earnings?

What is the sex and age of the horse?

What has he done at today's class and weight?

Top Money Horses

Learn the horse's average earnings per race this year, or if he has been out less than ten times this year, his average for this year and last year. Divide the total number of races run into the total money won. The result is his average per race. Where the difference between horses is not more than 10 percent, they may be considered a tie.

In theory, the top money horse is the best horse. In fact, the whole of the horse's record, the ability of his trainer, and the sagacity of his owner are packed into this figure; that is, the horse's average earnings per race. We usually need know little else as far as races over thirty days old are concerned.

Average money won is not of much value where the horse has not had ten races in the last year or two. Nor is it of much value when dealing with horses that have not averaged much: say, less than a few hundred dollars. On the other hand, great disparity between the top money horse and his nearest competitor is never to be underestimated. Say the top money horse averaged $800 per race and the next averaged $400. Such a gap needs a strong bridge.

The Gelding

When the race is a claimer for four-year-olds or older, a gelding has an edge over his running mates. In the case of two-year-olds, and also in high-class races, this does not seem to hold true. There the gelding seems to be at a disadvantage. The reason for this probably lies in the fact that an unsexed animal develops slower than others. Thus, he reaches his best form at five years old, and holds it up to eight or nine. In high-class races, the reason is likely to be the fact that owners reserve the very best horses for eventual breeding purposes.

It is probable that a gelding with average winnings of $300 per race is a match for a mare or horse averaging $450 to $500. This assumes that the gelding is between four and eight years old. A six-year-old gelding has a better chance than one that is four or five years old.

Ability in Today's Weight and Class

If a horse has been in the money at the weight he carries today, it is a sign that he may win at that weight. If he has been in the money in the class he is running today, it means he may win in that class. He need not have carried the weight in the class. It is sufficient that in each separately, he has been in the money. Also, it need not have been too recently. If it was in any of the races recorded in the chart, that is enough.

These points in a horse's record are not to be used alone. They merely tell us what he *can* do, not what he *will* do. Other considerations will decide how he is shaping up for today's race.

2. RECENT OUTINGS

This part concerns the horse's owner and trainer. Have these gentlemen been giving the horse the recent training that is necessary for the horse's best effort? This information is also found in the *Daily Racing Form*. Recent races and recent workouts are what count the most. Of the two, actual racing is the more important, but the closer a workout is to today's effort, the better it is for the horse. In claiming races, there is some evidence that a five-day gap between races is advisable, but that gaps of more than eleven days are not favorable.

Evaluating a Horse's Outings

Keep these four points in mind when you rate a horse's recent outings.

1. In claimers, a race in the last ten days and also a workout are highly desirable. In allowances and better, there are not many mounts that can have had such recent races. The higher the class of the race, the less frequently will the horses have run.

2. In claimers, there should have been at least a couple of races in the last thirty days and four races are even better. It is unlikely that races more than thirty days back or workouts more than ten days back are of any value in putting a horse into winning shape today. In higher-class races, the entrants will have had less racing.

3. A rest that took place a month or six weeks is a good sign. A horse is not likely to win immediately after a rest, but just as is the case with boxers, a rest period seems essential before commencing the heavy training that is needed to become a winner.

4. Races during the meet on the track where the horse runs today are important. The more often they have run in the meet the better it is, other things being equal. As is evident, however, this is not a consideration at the beginning of a meet since none of the horses will have qualified. About midway in the season it becomes important.

Occasionally, though not often at the major tracks, a horse may have had too many races in the thirty-day period or may have been kept on the track too long without a rest break. Just where to draw the line is difficult to say. Probably the safest rule to follow is this: When a horse has more than four races in the thirty days, or more than sixty days without a rest period, you must see in him a marked improvement in form. Owners are interested in making money. When a mount goes over ten days without a race, it is not illogical to suppose that the horse came off his last race sore or otherwise somewhat the worse for wear.

In high-class events, few of the horses will have had races during the thirty-day period. There would not have been openings enough for them. So, no races in the last ten days and one in thirty days is all right in such events. In very high-class races, a couple of races in a two or three-month period will often be enough, but there is no excuse for absence of workouts. A couple of races in the last ten days is a good sign.

Theoretically, a horse that has qualified under three or four points of the first group, and three or four points of the second group will do all right for himself today. But theory will not put money in your pocket! There are other considerations that will show whether or not the horse has really benefited by the training period. Then, too, we must check to be sure that his owner and the track stewards are being fair to him in the matter of weight and class. Very often he gets a break in that department and when he does, it covers a multitude of defects.

3. QUALITY IN RECENT OUTINGS

In checking up on the quality as opposed to the quantity of recent outings, we do not bother about what time he made at his workouts except in cases where the time was phenomenal. It is enough that he has had his share. It is what he did in his races that counts.

There are three groups of signs. It is not necessary that your choice qualify in each group, but if he does not qualify in *any* of them, only the mercy of his owner or the stewards can save him from defeat.

Group A Signs

All of these signs appear in the horse's last race.

1. A horse that ran in the money last time has a point in his favor. Or if he finished within a length of the winner, it is as good as being in the money.
2. It is a point in a horse's favor when he closed in the top half of his field in his last race.
3. A stretch gain last race (or in the absence of such a gain, leading the field from the first call to the wire) is a decisive sign that the horse is coming into his own.
4. The horse that bettered his position at each call last race is definitely on the up grade. Whether he bettered it in beaten lengths or by the passing of horses makes no difference.

Group B Signs

These three signs can qualify a horse even when Group A is negative. Still, very often, your horse will show something in both groups.

1. Overall gain last race is a very good sign. In number of beaten lengths, the gain of even ahead is better than no gain.
2. The fact that your horse passed horses is another good sign—the more he passed the better.
3. Trouble in the last race. Although trouble is not an asset, it can well explain the absence of an asset that we are looking for in the horse's last race. Horses often finish well despite bumps, being forced wide, jockey trouble, being forced to take up, and so on. Such horses have a point in their favor, probably even two points, because weights are fixed without reference to excuses.

Group C Signs

The third group of signs may also serve to show improvement and winning quality with or without favorable points in Groups A or B. In this case, we take the last two or three races.

1. A front breaker in his last three races has a definite advantage in a short race today, but usually has none at a mile and one-sixteenth or longer.
2. Improvement is indicated when a horse's position at the first call was better in the last race than it was the race before.
3. It is an added sign of progress when the horse was better in the last race at the finish than he was the race before.

The horse's betterment at the first call or at the finish may be either in terms of beaten lengths or in relation to the horse's position in the field. When improvement is apparent at each end and when the horse also qualifies under the fourth sign in the A Group, we have a very excellent combination.

The sign in question is where a horse in his last race bettered his position at each call. When it is the top money horse that shows this triple pattern, you are very likely to find your winner right there. Even though he is not the top money horse, if he has a speed rating for this meet at the track where he is running today, and if that speed rating is the best in the group, he is very likely to be the horse you want.

4. There is another way to detect improvement. It is a good one, but is not verified very often. This sign calls for a diagonal check of the calls in the horse's last three recent races. The horse must have been in a worse position at the first call three races back than he was at the second call in the race before

last. He also must have been in a worse position at that second call than he was in his last race at the third call. Furthermore, the next diagonal must qualify in the same way, beginning at the second call three races back and ending at the finish last race. Sample:

Diagonal Check Chart

4^4	4^3	3^2	2^1
7^6	8^5	8^4	6^3
9^{10}	9^8	9^7	9^6

In fact, where the improvement would be so apparent as it is in this sample graph, the horse is getting into very good form for a long race. Note that no matter how you read it—vertically, horizontally or diagonally—the improvement is to the right and up. For a short race, the position at the first call would usually not recommend the horse.

4. OFFSETS FOR POOR PERFORMANCE

Now we come to a point that I hinted at before listing the three groups of signs in recent races that can mark a winner. Any one of these groups of signs (A, B, C), or even all of them, may be negative, yet a horse that qualifies under our first two considerations may still win. The first two, as you will recall, are:

a. Potential or class in the horse, as evidenced by money won and by parallel performance; and

b. Quantity of recent training.

A horse will often show several of the signs in the A, B and C groups and still have assets in the following four points—

weight drop, class drop, more distance, unbeaten at class and weight. If this is the case, so much the better.

Let us look at each of them.

Drop in Weight

When a horse carries less weight today than he did in his last race, it is a very definite point in his favor. As a rule, the more he drops the better. I say "as a rule" because there seem to be horses that carry weight so well that a few extra pounds make them try all the harder. A drop of six pounds or more and a nice record in ability and practice points are required to offset a blank record in our three groups of signs for a winner.

Also note that a horse that runs today at, say, 115 pounds without an apprentice allowance, and who ran last time at 115 with an apprentice allowance is actually taking a five-pound weight drop. And keep an eye on the horse if his last jockey was in the fifth class and his present is in the first, second or third class.

Drop in Class

A class drop is often more important than a drop in weight, but both are important. When there is a drop in both class and weight, it is a very good indication of things to come.

In a case of drop in class, be sure to consider every horse in the race as running at the same claiming price, namely the highest price listed for any horse in the race. Owners sometimes put a lower price on their horses in order to get a lower weight assignment. But weight is seldom an offset for class. No matter how low any horse's price may be, he has to beat the most expensive horse there for you to collect on him.

More Distance

Where a horse is going more distance today, it is often a point in his favor. There is an exception to this rule in that fast-breaking, front-running horses can shorten their distance to advantage. It is the back runner and the stretch gainer that derive advantage from a lengthened distance.

Never Beaten at the Class and Weight

It is definitely in a horse's favor when he has never been beaten at the class and weight he is going at today or at a lower class and weight. It may well be that he has never run at so low a class and weight as he is running today and, for this reason, was never beaten at it. In either case, it is definitely a point in his favor. Note that we say class *and* weight, not class *or* weight.

Here ends our preliminary study of the points that are important in a prospect for the winner's circle. We will return to them again, so do not worry if you have not yet grasped their full import. Now let us turn our attention to the flip side of the coin—those signs that go against a horse, the topic of the next chapter.

6 SIGNS AGAINST A HORSE

Even if a horse has a great deal in his favor, there are points that work against him. Some points are not as important as their counterpoints that favor the winner because an owner need not let his steed run if he does not like the conditions.

FIVE SIGNS THAT GO AGAINST A HORSE

1. Running a Shorter Distance

Running at less distance today is usually a bad point, except that a drop from above a mile and one-sixteenth to that distance need not disturb you. Neither does shortening the distance work against a front runner.

2. Weight and Class Raises

Raises in either weight or class are sometimes problems, but if the raise is in one or the other and not in both, a good record in the winning points eliminates the objection. Males carrying over 118 pounds and females carrying more than 113 pounds are not good prospects unless their record shows that they have been able to end in the money at today's weight.

3. Stretch Gainers

Where a horse has lost in the stretch in recent races, one would be tempted from logic alone to distrust him. However, this does not seem to make much difference in either short or long races. Although a study of winners shows that stretch gainers have an edge, it does not follow that a horse otherwise qualified to win will not gain in the stretch today just because he has not been gaining recently. A past record of stretch gain is in a horse's favor but a record of non-gain does not go against him. This is especially true where the horse's speed rating made at this track in a recent race is better than that of his running mates. It is also true when he was leading at the stretch call in his last race and finished in the money (short or long races), or when he was leading at the pre-stretch call (long races) and ended in the money.

4. Slow Breakers

Slow breakers are at a decided disadvantage in short races and often possess an advantage in long ones. I do not mean that horses that usually reach the first call ten or more lengths back are worthy of consideration, even in long races. But if it is only five or six lengths back, it is nothing to worry about. Always remember, however, that remarkable overall gain can offset almost any amount of slowness at the start.

5. Going from Minor to Major Tracks

Horses transferring from a minor to a major track are at a decided disadvantage, as a rule. If the horse is not at least four races away from his minor track days, he is to be suspected. Nevertheless, a fine record can offset this defect. Conversely, a horse dropping from a major to a minor track is often a good bet. Do not hold an occasional race at a minor track against a horse that usually runs at the major tracks, but his record at the minor track will not have the same value as it would have had at a major track.

MORE UNFAVORABLE SIGNS

Three points that are logically against a horse include:

1. Increase in Weight

While this is not in a horse's favor, the defect can be offset by good points. A stretch gainer, or a horse that won his last outing handily or better, will not be bothered by a little extra weight—provided that he is not going up too much in class or extending his distance.

2. Jump in Class

Just as the case with weight, a moderate advance in class can be taken in stride by an improving horse. Notable advances are difficult to negotiate. Advances in both class and weight are very difficult to offset.

3. Off the Fair Circuit

Horses transferring from the fair circuit or from out of state usually need to develop form at major tracks before they rate a bet. Skip races where such an animal has an impressive record. About four races at the new track will give him a form you can trust. Note, however, that mounts that broke in front consistently at fairs or out of state are not bad prospects, especially if they broke in front at the first race on a major track. The odds are usually long enough to encourage even the cautious bettor.

7 OTHER FACTORS TO CONSIDER

I'm going to look at three factors in this chapter—post position, changes in odds, and speed ratings—before we move on to the nineteen signs of a winning horse. Let's start with a brief look at post position.

POST POSITION

One element in a race is pure chance—the horse's post position, which is chosen by lot. In short races, the post position seems to be of more importance than in long ones. In the short races, a fast breaker and front runner in an inside post position does seem to have the advantage. Positions two to four, however, are better than one, probably because both horse and jockey are subconsciously afraid of a brush against the rail.

Despite this, post position alone will not make a winner. However, when the competition is keen or where we are looking for convincing wins, it does help sometimes. Never choose or eliminate a horse on this consideration alone.

Concerning jockeys and jockey changes at the last minute, if your only reason for selecting one horse rather than another is the jockey, it is better to skip the race. If a horse has not come close to doing what he is asked to do today, and if the records of his recent races (or at least, weight or class drops) do not indicate that he is up to his best form today, the jockey cannot supply the oomph. All that the best jockey can do today is coax out of the horse all that he has in him.

CHANGES IN ODDS

Dropping odds on a horse is often an indication that, in the judgment of good horsemen and good private handicappers, the horse is ready for the winner's circle. Such changes do not always indicate that your selection of the previous evening is not the right one, but sometimes they do. When the changes are noted at the track, take another look at your *Daily Racing Form*. Probably you overlooked something.

Where the public handicappers favor a horse, it is to be expected that the odds will fall, and therefore no disturbing pattern is created. However, apart from that, there are three odds changes that merit a check.

1. Long Odds that Fall

When a horse is listed at long odds in the morning line and they fall noticeably at the track—say from 15 to 1 to 6 to 1 or less—those who know horses are betting on the steed.

2. Sudden Drops in Track Odds

Also, sudden drops in the track odds often indicate the same thing. Always in this odds business, we are talking about changes that are not explained by choices of the public handicappers, as well as when they are not explained by the jockey. Some jockeys have their blind admirers and a lot of these admirers would bet on the jockey even if he were aboard a draft horse!

3. A Raise in Track Odds

Conversely, a raise in track odds above the morning quotes may be indicative. Say a horse quoted at 3 to 1 in the morning is going to post at 5 to 1. You may have a good bet. The track handicappers who quote the morning odds know quite a bit about their business. Failure of the crowd to follow them usually means nothing. The fact that the shift is only moderate, say not much more than in the case quoted, means that a goodly number of careful bettors have been investing in the horse. Thus, you have two groups of able men favoring the steed. When you find this, recheck your *Daily Racing Form* if necessary, but make no change in your choice unless you detect an error in your judgment.

Strangely enough, in a surprising number of cases, you will be gratified to know that the very horse you have handicapped has turned up showing these odds changes.

SPEED RATINGS

So far I have said very little about the speed rating shown on a past performance record. This is not because I consider it without value, but because it can be very deceptive to the novice student of racing.

A racehorse seldom runs up to his best or even his most recent rating. A mount's courage, willingness and immediate preparation are the things that count. The best racehorse seldom works any harder on the track then he has to. The competition that the winner faces will determine his speed. If the elements we have discussed show that a horse is ready, he will go the distance at whatever speed his companions choose to extract from him. This means that whatever handicapping value the rating has is usually absorbed into the more tangible qualities we have been considering.

I say "usually" because sometimes the speed rating can be very useful—when it is recent and was made at today's track, today's distance and under today's track conditions, and when it looks good for the last three races. Moreover, when the *Daily Racing Form* shows in the background an exceptionally good series of ratings for a horse that has done nothing recently, it is often better to pass the race. On the other hand, where a mount has given evidence of recent improvement and we find exceptional speed ratings in his back history, we may have a very legitimate longshot play. Strangely enough, your choice will often prove to be the entrant with the best speed rating.

In high-class races it will not matter that the rating was not made at today's track, provided only that it is recent. Speed ratings made at minor or out-of-state tracks are of little value at the present oval. But when the fine ratings in a mount's back history were made at any top local track, respect them.

In a race where competition is keen, where two or three runners seem otherwise pretty equal, it is possible that the steed with the best recent rating is the best bet. But the person who bets in a businesslike way will pass up such races or will be satisfied with a $2.00 ticket.

If I somewhat belittle speed ratings. I do this deliberately, for I am convinced that one must have a knowledge of the whole handicapping picture before he can use the ratings as a starting point for handicapping. At the end of this book, I make some statements that will seem to contradict much of what I say here, but by then, you will know when to use them and when not to.

If you are not familiar with the use of the *Daily Racing Form*, you may be quite confused by now. This is only natural. Be patient: I will go on to clear things up, adding nearly everything you need to know about horseracing terms and interpreting the *Daily Racing Form*. I will also introduce a number of tables so that you can graphically see exactly what I mean concerning qualities to look for in a prospect for a bet. I have also included a table for computing at a glance the average money won per race. And along the way, I will point out shortcuts and easy, safe starting points.

But first, allow me to repeat the points you need to observe in a horse's past performance record. The next chapter reviews my main points in short form and in a practical order, and adds some fresh ideas to help you get a firmer grasp on the handicapping concepts in this book.

8 A SECOND LOOK: 19 SIGNS OF A WINNER

When making your betting decisions, always consider the following signs that a horse is a potential winner. For a quick review, I have listed them in a short form and in a practical order. Add to these signs your common sense and good judgment to fully enjoy a pleasurable and winning day at the track.

1. Average Earnings Per Race

Divide the total races into the total money earned by the entrant. Use the figures for this year only unless the horse has had less than ten races this year. In that event, use the totals for this year and last. The higher the average earnings, the greater the horse's potential or class.

2. Average Earnings Per Win

Some handicappers divide the total wins into the total money earned, as computed above. The higher the average, the better the potential. You can get a better index by allowing 8 points for each win, 5 for each place, 3 for each show and one for each fourth. Add the totals and divide into the total money won. (Others allot 12 points for each win, 4 for each place, 3 for each show and one for each fourth, and then divide that total into the total money earned. I do not use that criterion in this book.)

3. Sex and Age

The common abbreviations used to denote a horse's sex and age are: **c**, colt; **f**, filly; **h**, horse; **m**, mare; **g**, gelding; and **r**, ridgling. Geldings aged four to eight years have an edge in claimers $10,000 or under. The rest have the edge in better races and in lower age groups, with the male usually preferable to the female. All else being equal, geldings that are six or seven years old have an edge on those that are four or five years old.

4. Speed Rating Last Ten Days

Where the entrants have a race in the last ten days, the steed with the best rating has a point in his favor. In the better races, a race in the last ten days is uncommon. Speed ratings at minor tracks are of no value at major ones. Eastern speed ratings usually are not of value in the West, but outstanding ones should lead you to skip the races where such Eastern horses are entered, and vice versa.

5. Speed Rating Thirty Days

Both where there is no speed rating in ten days and where there is one, the best rating in thirty days merits consideration. In races better than $10,000, claimers use the ratings going back ninety days. In some events you will have to be satisfied with the best most-recent rating. This is especially true at the beginning of some meets.

Speed ratings are of special significance when the mount's rating for the last race is very good and is backed up by as good or better rating in the two previous outings.

6. Recent Races

Only recent races serve as a guide to the entrant's effective ability today. So, when we refer to signs in the entrant's last races, we mean those in the last month or six weeks for claimers and those in the last sixty to 120 days in the case of higher-class events.

7. Races Within Ten Days

Races within the last ten days are favorable in all races, but more frequent and valuable in claimers. Races closer than five days to today's event are not favorable as a rule, but within six to eleven days, they are good.

8. Workouts Within Ten Days

These are of great importance in all types of races. In claimers, a race or two during this period will substitute for the workout. The more workouts in this period, the better; and the closer a workout is to today's race, the better.

As a rule, the time made at a workout is of no consequence. Occasionally, however, one of the entrants will have turned in a phenomenal time. If this entrant is not your choice, skip the race or go light on your bet. Sometimes a horse lives up to his workout. If it is the mount of your choice that has turned in the workout, he merits a sizeable bet.

9. Races Within Thirty Days

Make this ninety or even 120 days for very high-class events. At least one race is needed, and up to four is good in claimers. Count the races you noted for the ten days.

10. Races this Track, this Meet

Only after the meet is well under way will this be of importance. Tracks differ, and the more often a horse runs in a meet, the better for him.

11. Top and Low Weights

The entrants with the highest weights are the officials' choices as the best entrants. Always consider them. The lowest weight, when twelve or more pounds under the top, merits a glance. Remember that females and the mounts of apprentices usually get a five-pound allowance. Add that to weight to determine true top and bottom. The low-weight horse may merit consideration when accompanied by notable class and/

or weight drops. Some handicappers consider the low weight a definite advantage when the track is heavy, muddy or sloppy.

12. Class and Weight Drops

These drops are of the greatest value when the entrant's last race is recent. The most significant drops are those from handicaps to allowances, or from either of these to claimers. But drops in claimer price are also very significant. Too great a drop in claimers sometimes indicates an unknown defect in the entrant, but there is no reason to suspect a drop of as much as $1,500. Occasionally, a considerable drop is noted after a long absence from the track. Such horses may force you to skip a race. Lacking a recent *Daily Racing Form,* you have no way of knowing what they will do today, yet their old record may look too good to consider them out of the running.

When the drop is in both class and weight, and if it is off a recent race, you have a good prospect for victory.

13. In the Money at the Class and Weight

If a horse has not been in the money at the class and weight for today or better, it is unlikely that he will win. He need not have carried the weight in the class—it is sufficient that he negotiated the weight in one race, and the class in another. This performance need not be recent. Any of the races given in the *Daily Racing Form* will do.

Of course, it is all the better if he has won in the class and also at the weight. It is still better when he has won carrying today's weight in today's class or better.

Lastly, an entrant that has not been beaten at today's class and weight, or that has never run so low in class and weight, naturally rates great consideration. I am referring to class and weight being negotiated in the same race.

14. In the Money Last Race

Entrants that were in the money last race, or were within a length or so of the winner, have given notice of improvement.

Even though they were not in the money, they usually should have beaten half the field in their last running.

15. Front Runners

A front runner is a horse that:

1. usually reaches the first call among the leaders; or
2. has been there the last three races; or
3. was there at least when he did win. These are excellent qualities for a short race and not to be despised in a long one.

To check on the recent improvement in such a runner, the following points on this list are important in evaluating his last race.

16. First at the End of the Free Run

The free run is the part of the race in which the entrant is usually given more or less free rein. It may be considered to end at the stretch in short races (under a mile), and at the prestretch or stretch (whichever is better) in longer events. The horse that was first at that point in his last race (even though he did not win) shows that he is getting ready for a win. Back runners may show this sign too, and in any type of horse, it is good. It is sufficient for back runners that they got to the wire within a length or less of the winner.

17. First at All Calls

The front runner is a well-trained horse up to his best form. He is a good prospect for a repeat if:

1. He gained in the stretch last race; or
2. He won convincingly though only holding his own or even losing somewhat in the stretch.

18. Less Distance Today

A shortening of the distance today as compared to the mount's last race is an advantage to a front runner, but it is very unfavorable to a back runner.

19. Back Runners

Slow-breaking back runners are prospects for victory, especially in long races—but only when certain signs have been observed in the entrant's recent races. There are as many as seven indications, any two or three of which may put the finger on the winner today.

1. **Overall Gain in Lengths**

    Last race only. Subtract the lengths behind the winner at the finish from the lengths behind the leader at the first call. The more lengths gained, the better. If your prospect won his last race, add the lengths by which he won. Even front runners can make an overall gain—so much the better when they do.

2. **Horses Passed**

    The more mounts a back runner passed last race, the better—but even one is better than none.

3. **Diagonal Improvement**

    Though relatively infrequent, this is a very favorable sign of things to come. The last three races are needed to see it, and the three must all be recent: within 40 days for claimers and 120 days for better races. When a rest period intervened, only races after the rest period are of value. In long races, three complete diagonals are essential. In short races, drop back one place. This will make your first diagonal appear in only two races and will eliminate the diagonal ending at the wire last race.

4. **Improvement First and Last Calls**

   Last two races. The entrant that was in a better position last race than he was the race before at both the first and the last call is showing improvement. Improvement at either call is good. This is also of great value in front runners.

5. **Better at Each Call**

   Last race only. Where a horse betters his position at each call, he is giving warning of preparedness. When this is accompanied by improvement at the first and last calls, so much the better. This is also good in front runners, though not usually essential.

6. **Stretch Gain**

   Either last race, two of the last three races, or usually in the races listed in the *Daily Racing Form*. This is important in the case of back runners, or at least those back runners that were not first at the end of the free run last race. It is not to be despised in any horse.

7. **More Distance**

   Lengthening the running distance today as compared with the last race is favorable to back runners, especially to those with overall and stretch gains last race. However, be cautious when the entrant is adding both distance and weight, even if he is dropping somewhat in class.

9 A SHORT METHOD FOR SELECTING THE WINNER

Most fans have very little time to study the races. Many do not have access to a *Daily Racing Form* until they reach the track. Still others are not inclined to make selection a labor. Enjoying the sport comes first and they are willing to overlook some good bets rather than tire themselves out by spending hours with the *Daily Racing Form*.

What most players want is a method that will keep them from losing money, yet will give them a selection in almost any race within ten to twenty minutes. To keep out of the red, we must collect on three out of ten bets and the odds must average at least 2.35 to 1. In other words, when we do collect, we must average $6.70 or better for $2.00 tickets.

Keeping Out of the Red
1. Collect on 3 out of 10 bets
2. Odds must average at least 2.35 to 1
This means we average $6.70 or better on $2.00 tickets

There are several approaches to handicapping that will give three wins in ten selections, and which will do that well and even much better in the matter of odds. But remember this important concept: *No method can be relied upon to produce any predetermined percentage of winners on any particular day.* Some days the method will produce over the percentage, others under. On occasion, it can fail six consecutive times—or it will pick three in a row. My advice to this: Be content with overall success. You should be well in the black after any series of sixteen or more plays.

Bear in mind, of course, that I cannot exercise judgment for you. All I can do is tell you what to seek and where to find it. The actual weighing of the facts turned up rests with you. Experience will correct your errors, so make the most of it.

In war, it is "the army that gets there first with the most" that wins the battle. On the track, it is "the mount with the most" that gets there first.

But which mount has the most?

HOW TO FIND THE MOUNT WITH THE MOST

Any acceptable method of handicapping must be based on three factors: class, speed and action. The mount with the highest class, the best speed record, and the most impressive recent action (outings) is certainly the best bet. Were it as simple in fact as it is in theory there would be no bad handicappers. It is by no means so simple.

First of all we must learn to spot class, speed and action. This is not difficult, but it is only after we have learned this that our problem begins. Very often no one mount is best in all three and, as a rule, two or more mounts share all three in more or less equal amounts. Thus selecting no longer becomes a problem of mere observation but a matter of judgment—a judgment that you must make personally and for each race.

Furthermore, other elements can so greatly modify class, speed and action that any or all three may be nullified to the point where we must consider a horse that is under the top in class, speed or action. These modifying considerations are weight, distance, and form.

1. ELIMINATE RACES AND MOUNTS

To be most practical and yet as quick and accurate as possible, follow these three rules. They will eliminate from consideration certain races and, in all races, certain mounts.

a. Make Your Selections After Scratches Have Been Posted

By making your selections after scratches have been made, you will avoid wasting your time on mounts that may not even run.

b. Skip Mounts With No Recent Race—Thirty Days for Claimers, Sixty Days for Better

Skip races where some entrants are taking notable class drops but have no recent races. Pass up mounts from out-of-state tracks and those coming in off the fair circuit. As a rule, give these horses three or four races at a local major track before considering them. Skip maidens and mounts just off a maiden win. It is probably all right to bet on a mount off a maiden win if the race in which he broke his maiden status was at a speed rating lower than he had earned in a previous race.

c. Pass Races for Two-Year-Olds and Maidens

Quick selections for turf or off tracks are not likely to be good bets. Skip the great classics where the purse is exceptionally high, as well as races under six furlongs and those over a mile and a quarter. Despite this recommendation, if you still want to play these races, bet lightly.

Judge turf and other off track entrants by the records they made at today's distance and track condition.

In the case of two-year-olds, the one with the best workout time is probably the best bet.

In races under six furlongs, choose the fastest breaker.

In extra long runs, the horse that has been in the money at the distance is not too bad a choice, especially if his last race was a long one in which he gained ground somewhere along the line.

Sometimes a young horse with a bad race after two or three good workouts and which has had no workout after the bad race is a good longshot bet. The mount should have made good time from the gate in a workout and a good breezing workout helps. The trainer is satisfied with his horse or he would not have run him right back.

2. CHECK THE CLASS, SPEED AND ACTION OF THE REMAINING MOUNTS

Now that you have eliminated certain races, it is time to check the speed, class and action of the remaining mounts.

a. Check the Mount's Speed

Speed is easiest to ascertain. The mount with the highest rating last time out gets a point. You may put a pencil stroke in the form margin for each point till you get used to handicapping.

The mount with the highest rating (not counting the last race) during the last sixty days deserves a point and so does the entrant with the best backlog of ratings. A good rating thus backed up by better ratings is a fine omen.

The horse that turned in an impressive workout time within the last fourteen days rates a point.

Pay no attention to ratings made at minor tracks and be cautious of ratings earned at out-of-state tracks.

Skip ratings made on the turf.

Adjust or skip those secured on tracks affected by the weather.

I do not mean to belittle out-of-state ratings at major tracks; they often mean more than in-state ratings. But until the mount earns competitive in-state ratings, he usually just does not have what it takes.

b. Check the Mount's Class

There exists the class in which the owner thinks his horse belongs. This is evidenced in his backlog of races, with the lowest claimers at the class bottom and the handicaps at the top. The owner's idea of class and the horse's real class need not agree. If the mount has not been in the money at the class, the owner is pitching him too high.

The very simplest method of establishing real, cashable class is to divide the total races into the total money earned. Where the difference between horses is not more than 10 percent, consider them equal. Give the top money horse two points and his nearest competitors one point each.

1. Give a point to the mount with the highest class last race.
2. Give a point to the horse that ran in the highest class during the last sixty days.
3. Give a point for the best backlog in class.

The very fact that the mount raced in a higher class is in his favor, but if he was in the money at the class, it is of still more importance.

c. Check the Mount's Action

Action means recent races and workouts. In claimers, the races for the last thirty or forty days are all that count. In better races, we may go back much farther, ninety or even 120 days. The better a horse the less racing he needs—or for that matter, the less chance will he have had to race.

There must always have been a workout (or a race) in the last ten days. The closer a race or a workout is to today's event, the better.

Give a point for a race within eleven days but not closer than five days.

Give a point to mounts with an impressive race last time out or gave evidence of racing improvement.

When races are impressive in two or more ways, give extra points. The following races are evidently impressive.

- First all the way.
- First or second at the stretch call, gained in the stretch and won.
- Races won breezing, easily or handily—that is, when the horse won by three or more lengths.
- Better at each call.
- Notable overall gain either in lengths, horses passed, or both.

TWO FACTORS THAT MAKE A HORSE IMPRESSIVE

Though they may not appear to be important at first glance, the following factors are impressive:

Even if the mount weakened or died in the stretch, it was first at the stretch call. If no mount was first, then the one best at the stretch call deserves a point.

The mount bettered his position at the first two calls in his last two races. The betterment must be in both position and lengths (unless, of course, he was first, in which case lengths only are needed). Moreover, the improvement must follow an inverted Z pattern. For example:

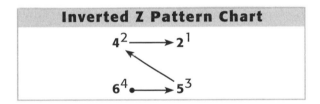

In case the mount at the second call, last race, was further back than second, and/or three or more lengths behind the leader, then he must have been first or within a neck of first at the stretch call. For an inverted Z improvement, allow two points.

When, in the last three races, you have observed the Diagonal Check Chart (shown again below for easy reference), give the mount a point.

Diagonal Check Chart			
4^4	4^3	3^2	2^1
7^6	8^5	8^4	6^3
9^{10}	9^8	9^7	9^6

THREE REASONS TO THROW OUT THE LAST RACE

Remember that sometimes, the last race must be thrown out—it must not be given any more value than an unimpressive workout. The following races should be eliminated and we should drop back one race.

Where the previous race or two led you to expect a fine showing and the mount turned in a miserable one. Sometimes the trouble that caused the bad showing is detected, sometimes it is not; but whether detected or not, throw out the race.

Where the last race was not true to form and was also no good. For example, where a back runner was among the leaders at the first call or a front runner trailed the field.

Bad showings on the turf or on tracks slowed by the weather. If the showing was good, the speed rating must be adjusted. In the case of turf, I do not suggest any safe adjustment. In short races, add 3 points for good, 8 for slow, 10 for sloppy, 15 for muddy, and 20 for heavy tracks. In long races, double these figures. But in no event consider the speed rating resulting from any adjustment to be greater than the mount has ever made on a normal track. When adjustments would put the rating higher, just take the best rating ever actually made.

Now, the mount with the most strokes in the margin is as good a bet as you can select in short order. If he has four strokes more than his nearest rival, you can put 10 percent of your racing fund on his nose. When your selection is a front runner, you can feel more confident of victory in a short race. In long races, the mount with the power for overall gain usually deserves to be the favorite. I do not mean to suggest that the aspects of a race that have I referred to here are of equal importance. They are not. Furthermore, these various aspects have different values in different circumstances. Experience will teach you.

WHEN TO SKIP A RACE

While it is foolish to bet against the mount with the most, you will sometimes have to skip the race or bet very lightly. No matter how good or ready a horse may be, weight can ruin his chance to win. Look for these things:

If your selection has never been in the money at today's weight or higher, pass the race.

It is rare that a horse can negotiate an advance in both class and weight. If your selection is up in both, he must have run in the money at both today's class and today's weight. But he need not have negotiated both class and weight in the same race.

Front runners can shorten their run without bad effects. Back runners are often helped by extending their run. On the other hand, it is difficult for a front runner to be successful at more distance, or for a back runner to win shortening his race. Of course, I am not talking about stake class horses here, only horses in allowances or under.

Entrants that are advancing in class, weight and distance rarely win. Skip the race when your favorite is this horse.

THE NEVER-BET RULE

Never bet against the horse that seems best to you—and never bet on him if he has not done or come near doing what he is asked to do today. He must have been in the money at the class, at the weight, at the distance, on this track or one equal to it. But he need not have done all these things or even any two of them in any one race.

At this second stage in your study of handicapping, I recommend that you mark your *Daily Racing Form* for about ten days, as indicated in this short method. This exercise will impress upon your mind the important points and will aid you to rightly interpret the still shorter approaches I will now address.

If this multi-step, longer method is more than you feel up to, try the 12-Point Method, an even shorter way to choose a winner, that I discuss in the next section.

10 THE 12-POINT METHOD: AN EVEN SHORTER WAY TO CHOOSE THE WINNER

If the short method that I outlined in the last chapter has too many points for you to comfortably follow, or if you simply don't have enough time to go through its steps, try this 12-Point Method for selecting winning horses.

THE 12-POINT METHOD FOR RATING A WINNER

1. Give one point to the mount with the highest average earnings per race this year.

2. Give one point to the mount with the highest average earnings per race this year and last year.

3. Give one point to the mounts that won or were within two lengths of the winner in the last race.

4. Give one point to the mounts that gained in the free run—those that were in a better position at the stretch call than they were at the first call.

5. Give one point to each mount that bettered its position at the first call last race, as compared to the race before. *(continued)*

THE 12-POINT METHOD FOR RATING A WINNER *(continued)*

6. Give one point to the mounts that were first at the first call. If none was first, then give one point to the mount closest to first at the first call, provided it was not more than two lengths from first.

7. Give one point to the mount with the best speed rating last race.

8. Give one point to the mount with the best speed rating during the last 60 days, not counting the last race.

9. Give one point to the top weight mount, if 116 pounds or more.

10. Give one point to the low weight mount, if 110 pounds or less.

11. Give one point for a race in the last ten days.

12. If the mount with the top speed rating last race had a worse break in that race than it had in the race before, give it a point.

HOW TO INTERPRET A HORSE'S POINTS

If any mount has seven or more points and is at least two points above his nearest rival, you have a good bet. If none qualifies under this rule, skip the race or choose the one with the most points and bet moderately. We recommend again that for a week or so you mark your form as directed. It is the third step in your study of handicapping.

THE ONE-TWO SYSTEM

If even this 12-Point Method is too much, you are in the market for the One-Two System. The chart below outlines the five principles to follow. Try this for a few days and compare your results with those at the track.

THE ONE-TWO SYSTEM

1. Bet only when a qualifying horse has had a race in the last ten days.

2. Choose the top weight mount or the top money horse or the entrant with the highest speed rating during the last ninety days.

3. Bet to win in short races when the mount was first at the first call; or within two lengths of first at the first call; and first or within a neck of first at the stretch call last race.

4. Bet to win in long races when the mount was first at the stretch call last race; or when it gained at each call last race and finished in the money; or when it was first at all calls last race.

5. Skip races where this one-two pattern is absent and be patient. You will have dry runs but overall you will do all right.

In the next section, we will look at some more methods that will allow you to choose a mount quickly. Or where that is not possible, to skip the race or have recourse to the fuller knowledge that you have gained up to this point.

11 FIVE SUCCESSFUL TYPES OF BETTORS

Joe, a bookie who has been in business for twenty years, had only one client who beat him. Joe bet only mounts that were first at the first call in their last race, provided the race was not more than ten days back and provided no other mount in today's race broke as well last time out. He most likely bet only on races under one mile.

Tom always skips the first three races. On the rest of the races, he bets on the mount that shows the most improvement at the first call last race as compared to the same call race before last. Both races must be recent. Tom is satisfied with the results. He prefers races of one mile or more. Occasionally, however, a good bet is often found in one of the first three races.

Then there is Bill who bets only the entrant that was first or within a neck of first at the stretch call last race. The last race must be not more than fifteen days back and if that far back, there should be a workout within ten days. Bill seems to be doing all right.

Jerry, somewhat more conservative, chooses the mount preferred by Tom. But in short races, he insists that the mount must have been within a neck of first or better at the first call, and must have bettered that position at the stretch call. For long races (one mile or more), Jerry requires his choice to have been not more than five lengths behind the leader at the first

75

call, and within a length of the leader or better at either the stretch call or the wire.

Russ, who likewise uses a mount's last race as a basis of his choice, points out that the following patterns in a last race are indicative of the improvement required for a win:

1. The horse that bettered his position at each call.
2. The horse that dropped back at the second call but bettered his position at each succeeding call.
3. The horse that bettered his position at each call but lost ground in the stretch.
4. The horse that lost ground between the first and second calls, and then gained to the stretch but fell back in the stretch.

In any of these cases an improvement at the first call over the mount's position at that call in the previous race adds value to the pattern.

When the mount with the best speed rating during the last 90 days shows one of these four patterns, Russ bets on that horse. If no mount shows any of the patterns, in short races, he takes the mount with the highest speed rating if he has at least bettered his break; and in long races, if he has gained in either the pre-stretch or the stretch.

While these five men bet only on mounts that show signs of being ready, only one of them bets every mount that qualifies, irrespective of class, speed, money earned or anything else. That man is Joe. He has had long, dry periods, but has hit enough longshots to come out on top.

All the other bettors demand that the mount be running in class. By "class," I mean the ability to carry weight at the speed needed to win. The mount that has carried the greatest weight at the highest speed possesses the highest class. And he is the least risky bet if he has shown any of the patterns pointed out by Russ in his last race. Indeed, if he is notably superior in class to his running mates, he is a dangerous competitor, even though in his recent outings he has shown little or nothing.

THREE TYPES OF PLAYERS

When one uses a "quickie" method of selection, bets to win are liable to be rather risky. There are three types of players: the professional, the occasional player, and the addict.

1. Professional

The professional makes his living betting and goes to the track nearly every day. He can well be satisfied with two or three bets in an afternoon. He can afford the time to check carefully, so he is not interested in quickie handicapping methods.

2. Addict

The addict is a constant player without control of himself. He acts under compulsion and should see a psychiatrist.

3. Occasional

The occasional player has his regular work to do and gets to the track once a week or, in many cases, less frequently. He wants to enjoy himself, yet make a little money. It is all right for him to use the quickie method, but he must supplement it with rules that will keep his odds in line. Otherwise he will come away in the red.

If you are an occasional player, the conservative bettor's investment method is probably the most satisfactory for you. It consists of four betting guidelines.

GUIDELINES FOR CONSERVATIVE BETTORS

- Mounts going to post at 2 to 1 or less, bet to win.
- Mounts going to post at more than 2 to 1 but less than 4 to 1, bet win and place.
- Mounts going to post at between 4 to 1 and 9 to 1, bet across the board.
- Mounts going to post at 10 to 1 or better, bet win and show.

12 HOW TO ANALYZE SIGNIFICANT RACES, CLASS AND SPEED

Significant last races are often referred to as those in which the mount served warning. Not all handicappers, however, mean the same by "served warning." A significant race last time does not mean victory today. No last race is significant if it is too far back for its effects to carry over till now. A race over eleven days old is hardly a safe guide to the mount's readiness today if we are dealing with claimers. In high-class events, one can go back farther, a month certainly, maybe more, because owners of such horses train their mounts assiduously between events.

The following is a list of races that are significant and are rightly called races in which a mount served warning. I have inserted a suggested symbol that you can use for each type of race.

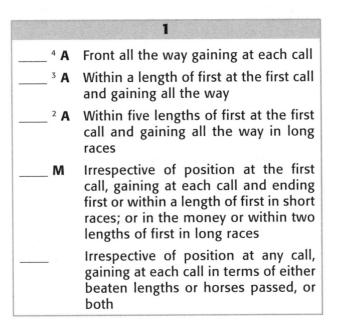
RACES IN WHICH A MOUNT SERVED WARNING

1. THE MOUNT GAINED AT EVERY CALL

1
____ ⁴ **A** Front all the way gaining at each call
____ ³ **A** Within a length of first at the first call and gaining all the way
____ ² **A** Within five lengths of first at the first call and gaining all the way in long races
____ **M** Irrespective of position at the first call, gaining at each call and ending first or within a length of first in short races; or in the money or within two lengths of first in long races
____ Irrespective of position at any call, gaining at each call in terms of either beaten lengths or horses passed, or both

These five races are listed in the order of their significance, the last item being the least valuable, though not to be spurned, especially in long races where the position at the first call is worse than the mount's normal. Even in short races, it is good where the mount is usually a front breaker. In no event is consistent overall gain without some significance.

2. THE MOUNT GAINED AT EVERY CALL TO THE STRETCH, BUT FELL BACK IN THE STRETCH.

2	
¬ 4	From all the way to the stretch.
¬ 3	Within a length of first at the first call and bettering his position at each call to the stretch.
¬ 2	Within five lengths of first at the first call and bettering his position at each call to the stretch, being first or within a length of first at the stretch call in long races.
¬ M	Irrespective of the position at the first call, gaining at each call to the stretch, being first or within a length of first there, and ending in the money or within two lengths of first.
¬	Gaining at each call to the stretch irrespective of the position at any call.

Again, these races are listed in the order of their significance, with the last one not to be spurned if his break was worse than normal, the normal being a front breaker for short races and a medium-fast breaker for long ones. Even without reference to previous races, this consistent gaining of ground occasionally has its value.

3. THE MOUNT LOST GROUND BETWEEN THE FIRST AND SECOND CALL BUT BETTERED HIS POSITION AT EACH CALL THEREAFTER.

3	
v····4	Front at the first call, loss of ground at the second, first thereafter.
v····3	Within a length of first at the first call, loss of ground at the second, bettered at each call thereafter.
v····2	Within five lengths of first at the first call, loss of ground at the second, and bettered his position at each call thereafter in long races.
v····1	Irrespective of position at the first call, loss of ground at the second and betterment at each succeeding call, ending in the money or within two lengths of it in long races.
v····	Worsening at the second call and improving at each call thereafter, irrespective of position or lengths. This is significant if the break is worse than normal as noted above, and seldom to be entirely disregarded.

4. THE MOUNT LOST GROUND BETWEEN THE FIRST AND SECOND CALL, GAINED BETWEEN THE SECOND AND THIRD, THEN LOST IN THE STRETCH.

4	
v¬ 4	First at first and third calls.
v¬ 3	Within a length of first or better at the first and third calls.
v¬ 2	Within a length of first or better at the first call (short races) or the same at the third call.
v¬1	Irrespective of positions at first or third, ending in the money (any race) or within two lengths of it (long races).
v¬	This pattern irrespective of position at any call.

5. A RACE IN WHICH THE MOUNT GAINED GROUND ANYWHERE AFTER THE FIRST CALL

5	
—S	Gain between the first and second call is good for a short race today.
—L	Gain in the prestretch run or in the stretch run is good for a long race today.

6. CONSISTENT MOUNTS

6	
FR	Despite his last race, a consistent front runner is a mount to consider in any short race.
OAG	A mount that usually makes an overall gain between the first call and the wire always merits consideration.

7. IMPROVEMENT OVER LAST RACE

7	
bb	Better break (better at the first call).
di	Diagonal improvement. (See *Diagonal Improvement Chart*)
Z	Inverted Z improvement. (See *Inverted Z Chart*)

When any of these patterns show in a mount running today, he should be in the money if he is the highest class entrant in the event. Whether he will or not depends first on his class differential. If his class differential is high enough, it can bring him in, even with the minimum in a recent race; or sometimes, with nothing in recent races; and occasionally, when he entirely lacks recent races. In most races, however, the best mounts are close enough in class to have needed recent races to segregate them.

SPOTTING THE HORSE WITH THE HIGHEST CLASS

Several methods can be used to spot the horse with the highest class.

1. W   WEIGHT

When he is three or more pounds above his nearest rival, the top weight mount is the entrant that, by track handicapping rules, is considered the highest-class mount in the event. On rare occasions the mount which in previous races carried the most weight, even without success, will be lightly rigged today. Such an entrant can be the class of the race. By this method, the mount that has carried the greatest weight in the highest class race is the class in today's event.

2. M   MONEY

When his average earnings per race are 20 percent or better above his nearest rival, the top money mount is the one that has been most consistently running in a class for which he is best fitted. His earnings further show that he can handle competition in his class.

3. T   TIME

The mount with the best time as adjusted to today's weight is the one that logic alone would fix as having the highest class. In the last analysis, class is the ability to speed under weight over a given distance. Therefore, the mount that made today's distance in the fastest time at today's weight should be the class of the race. When the mount is running under his record weight adjustment, he is usually safe enough. When he is running above the record weight, the adjustment needs verification. He should have carried today's weight successfully at another distance.

4. CL   CLASS

The mount within a length of the winner or better in the highest class race has some claim to being the class of the event. He is also a candidate if he has done very well in a notably higher-class race than have his companions in their races.

5. R   SPEED RECORDS

Classifying mounts based on their speed records (with these adjusted for all tracks where needed) is often the quickest method of selecting the highest-class entrant. Further, where the differential is notable, it is the safest.

R3 The mount with the best speed rating in the last thirty days.

R6 The mount with the best speed rating for the previous sixty days.

R9 The mount with the best rating in races over ninety days back.

There are certain problems with speed ratings. However, for our purposes we will consider the ratings at the major tracks to have the same value. The rating that we are interested in is the rating that the horse made irrespective of the distance run or the weight carried.

It may be that ratings for races under six furlongs are to be suspected when we are considering races of a mile or more. However, from six furlongs and up, the distance is not important.

There is the problem of adjustments for off tracks, some of which we have already suggested. It is well known that certain horses do relatively better in the mud than they do on a fast track. It is unlikely that making an adjustment that would give the horse a higher rating than he has ever made on a fast track is true. Where the horse wins only in the mud, if his adjusted rating would exceed the best he ever did on a fast track, it is safer to consider his adjusted rating the best that he has ever made on a fast track.

In the case of mounts that have done well on fast tracks, the adjustments for mud often give them ratings far higher than they ever actually made. Despite this, they indicate willingness and power under adversity. Tracks made worse by the weather have the same effect as added weight on an animal. In many races, the mount with the highest adjusted rating proves that in today's race, he is in fact possessed of the highest class.

Where the mount possesses the highest rating (even if an adjusted one) for the three periods we consider, there is no doubt but that he is the highest in class. It is not often that this situation occurs.

If the mount is best in any two of the periods, we have to be satisfied with that. Where he is definitely best in only one of the periods, it is best to demand evidences of class, as apparent in the other criteria we have studied.

FOUR CONSIDERATIONS
FOR SPEED RATINGS

In considering speed ratings, the higher they are the more leeway exists. Let's look at the chart.

SPEED RATINGS
1. Ratings under 75 are unreliable except on mud.
2. Between 75 and 95, a two-point differential is of value.
3. Between 95 and 99, there is no differential.
4. In the 100s where there is not a four-point differential, there is none.

In fact, once a mount hits 100, he can and often does whatever is requested of him. I am talking about unadjusted ratings, made on a fast track but not on the turf. If there are two or more mounts that have hit the 100-mark, one of them will usually win—but which one is hard to say!

13 A SIMPLIFIED WINNING METHOD

I have a friend who seems to be rather typical of the average racing fan. He does not get to the track very often and when he does go, he bets on every race—yet he is averse to making selection a labor. Moreover, he does not relish losing money. I close this book with an account of his method of selection because I have a feeling that many readers share his attitude.

Frank has been a diligent follower of the Sport of Kings for several years, and he has great respect for the handicapping ability of that section of the public that bets heavily enough on any race to make a notable impression on the odds. He maintains that, whereas the favorite wins 35 percent of the time, the first or second favorite will place in 85 out of 100 runs. In some instances, the odds on the second and third favorites differ less than $1.00, which is not enough to separate them. In such a case, the three going to post at the lowest odds are considered.

Frank lets the fans do his basic handicapping. About five minutes before post time, he takes out his form and considers only the two or three mounts which are the favorites at that time. The one he chooses, he will bet to place—no matter what the odds. He eliminates from all consideration every mount except these two or three. Of these, the one with the highest average earnings per race gets one point. The one that has run carrying the greatest weight in the highest class gets one point. Class is thus determined from two aspects. When possible, Frank assigns a third point to the mount with the most significant last race.

In events six furlongs or under, he gives the point to the mount that was first or nearest first at the first call. In seven furlongs or mile races, it goes to the mount that was within three lengths of first or better at the first call, and which improved his position at the second call. In a mile and seventy yards, it goes to the mount that was within four lengths of first or better at the first call, and which bettered his position at the second or third calls. In the mile and one sixteenth, Frank gives the point to the mount that was within four lengths of the leader or better at the first call, and that was within a length or better of the leader at the stretch call.

In longer races, the point goes to the mount that gained in the stretch or that showed a notable overall gain of four lengths or more, provided he ended in the money or within three lengths of the winner. The fourth point goes to the mount with the best speed rating in the last thirty days.

Frank places his bet on the mount with the most points.

He has done very well. He cannot get to the track more than twenty days in the year. All twenty days are in the summer and fall, which are probably the best seasons for betting. He bets $10.00 on every race. Occasionally, Frank is in the red for the day. Often he hits as high as seven out of eight races. On the overall picture, he pays all his expenses and makes a little on the side. By the way, if he misses two races in a row, he bets to win on the third.

I am not saying that this method is the most rewarding, but I do say that if you are not willing to learn all there is to know about this sport, you will do far better imitating Frank than you will following any tipster or hunch. Furthermore, and this is most important, there are days on which you will kick yourself no matter what method you use. Just remember that and stick to your guns. You will come out all right in the long run.

By the way, Frank does not play two-year olds or maidens, nor does he play when the mounts are equal in points.

14

7 RULES FOR MANAGING YOUR BANKROLL

In the matter of your funds for race playing, I make a rather startling statement, but one that is nonetheless true: If a person cannot go to the races with $100 in his pocket and play the rest of his life without adding capital from any source but the races, he should give up racing as a means of picking up a few extra dollars!

I am not saying that he should give up racing, but I do say that he should consider it merely as a sport and one for which he expects to pay, just as he does any other form of entertainment. Even at that, he is better off at racing than at other expensive pastimes. Sometimes he will leave money ahead; other times broke. At least he will have a chance to get something back at the races.

A few common sense rules can make that first $100 work for you through the years.

1. Be sure the money you take to bet is all yours, and that no one will suffer if you lose it. Never borrow, even during the races. This rule goes for all types of horseplayers.

2. Never accept money from anyone to bet for them, not even from your wife or family. The only exception to this rule is where the person picks a specific horse and states exactly how you are to play

him and what you are to bet on him. The reason for these rules may not be evident, so let me give it to you. A player does not mind losing his own money, on his own judgment, but he does not like to have others lose on his decisions. This psychological state makes the player too cautious and thus clouds his judgment.

Conversely, it is all right to give a few bucks to someone who has gone broke at the track. Such lads will be those who have not read this book or perhaps are the type that cannot profit by it. They are in the class that created the saying, "All horse players die broke."

Like most sayings, this saying is general and therefore false. It should read, "Those who gamble on horses, or anything else, will end up broke if they do not quit when they're ahead." The only gambler who does not lose in the long run is the man who runs the joint, or in the case of horses, the bookie or the track.

THE 7 RULES FOR MANAGING YOUR BANKROLL

Now back to that $100 in capital. (Of course, you can choose your own starting bankroll, but I find this $100 suggestion a good place to start.) One needs training and restraint to observe faithfully, and for all time, the rules here given. Only by observing them will you be able to manage your funds wisely.

1. The 10% rule

Never bet more than 10 percent of your racing funds on any race—and do not bet even that much where there is more than one outstanding contender.

2. The 2% Rule

If you wish to bet on every race, do not bet more than two percent of your funds on the types of races that this book points out as usually being unpredictable.

3. Managing Losses Sensibly

Never double your bets when you lose. Stick to the 10 percent maximum. If your racing bankroll falls below $50, skip all unpredictable races.

4. Managing Your Racing Bankroll

Keep your racing bankroll separate, but when it is over $100, you may use part of it to pay your incidental racing expenses. When it reaches $600, put $500 aside as a reserve and start over again with the balance. When the second $100 reaches the $500 mark, continue playing with that sum and do as you wish with the winnings. Using the 10 percent rule, a $500 bankroll makes your maximum wager $50. Most players should not advance beyond the $50 maximum wager. The risk of losing what seems to them to be a great sum of money will upset the indifference needed for good judgment.

5. Do Your Own Handicapping

Choose your own horses and pay no attention to tips. As a rule, you can know as much about the horses as anyone else. Often, your judgment will be better than that of the trainer. After all, trainers are often prejudiced. Pay no attention to other handicappers, professional or amateur. Horseplayers, like fishermen, are often braggarts. If they were as good as they say, they would all own yachts! There are players who do own yachts, but they are the ones who kept their mouths shut. If you close your ears to those giving tips, your lack of self-confidence will vanish and your judgment will be better. If you close your mouth to those seeking tips, your human respect will not be put to a test.

6. Do Not Give Tips

Never give a tip on one horse to anyone. If you are asked and want to be sociable, mention the two or three horses you think are best, and add, "At the proper odds, one of these would be a good bet." Nevertheless, you will do better never to give anyone the impression that you can handicap.

7. Do Not Try To Get Rich Fast

This observation really should not be necessary in the face of the 10 percent rule, but I will make it anyway. *Don't try to get rich fast!* Betting must be operated like any other business. Be very happy if you clear 10 percent per day on your investment, on the average. One can do that and better. It is doubtful that you could do as well in anything else.

The 10 percent of your bankroll rule will work in your favor when you have a run of good judgment. And it will protect you when your judgment is faulty. Starting with $100, it takes 27 consecutive losses to break you, and that many in a row is just not possible when you have some knowledge of racing.

I have taken $100 as the ideal initial bankroll, but you can start with $20 and still have ten chances to get going. Or if you have so much money that $1,000 or $10,000 or more to you is like $100 to me, start with those higher amounts.

15 ABSOLUTELY ESSENTIAL HANDICAPPING RULES

The following rules will recapitulate certain aspects of handicapping which are absolutely essential to being a winner.

1. **Keep What You Do at the Track Strictly to Yourself at All Times, Before and After**
   Even during a race, keep a poker face. Only those who are not sure of thcmselves betray their thoughts and feelings. You are simply not ready for successful wagering until you can control your tongue and your emotions.

2. **Never Bet Money That is Not Your Own, or Money That is Your Own But is Needed Elsewhere**
   Never depend on race winnings to get you out of a hole. Establish a racing fund with money you are free to throw away and use only that fund for betting. Never bet more than 10 percent of the fund on any race—and never bet even that much unlcss you are quite certain that your selection will do at least what you are wagering he will do.

3. **Make Your Own Selections**
   Your ears are useless in this field. Your eyes are essential. Let experience correct your errors. No

one can teach you how to play the horses. It is a matter of judgment. The better and more secure your judgment becomes, the better will be your results.

4. **It is Not Possible to Make a Selection for a Safe Win Bet in Most Races**
    However, there are few races in which a good handicapper cannot spot a mount that has what it takes to land in the money. In such cases, if you frequently go to the races, you will not mind passing up the race. But if you get there only occasionally, you probably will want to place a wager.

5. **Never Bet Against the Mount That Seems to You Most Likely to Win**
    Nevertheless, if you do not have full confidence in your selection, do not hesitate to make a place or even a show bet. It is better to collect show money than no money! I advise making $2.00 bets for six months. Get to the track at least twenty times in that period. Check the *Daily Racing Form* every day for the six months. Whether you bet or not, make one selection for each race. After the race, watch what the winner had that your selection did not have.

This book tells you what to watch for. It cannot analyze each race for you, but it does give you everything necessary for success at the races. With this information, if you lose $100 on the horses, please take my advice and admit to yourself that you are a poor handicapper, a person that can neither make a living nor a killing at the track. Know yourself! If you become a good handicapper, you will not be in the red more than two days in six. If you are not a good handicapper, horseracing is still a good sport, but it can be an expensive one unless you stick to $2.00 wagers.

 # CONCLUDING REMARKS

To me horseracing is a rewarding hobby, which has been my approach to playing the races. It has been profitable, both monetary and from the people I have met through the years. The camaraderie between us horseplayers is strengthened because of our common enemy, the pari-mutuel machines. The good friends I have made are legion.

When I say that I have made money on the horses, don't get the idea that a fortune is involved. I have made some money but not a living off the track. I have been conservative in my program, and recommend that you be conservative in your program. Be realistic and view your betting activity as recreation. Never get involved for more than you can afford and you will find, as I have, that you can spend more enjoyable hours at the track than you ever can spend fishing, hunting, gardening, or all the myriads of things people call pastimes and hobbies.

And for a lot less money. Really!

 **GLOSSARY**

Across the Board

A bet on a horse to win, place or show. "Bet *across the board* on mounts going to post at between 4 to 1 and 9 to 1."

Age

January 1 is deemed to be the legal birth date for all thoroughbreds. "The common abbreviations used to denote a horse's sex and *age* are: **c**, colt; **f**, filly; **h**, horse; **m**, mare; **g**, gelding; and **r**, ridgling."

Allowance

A reduction in weight that a horse carries based on certain race conditions such as an apprentice jockey or a female mount racing against males. "Remember that females and the mounts of apprentices usually get a five-pound *allowance*."

Apprentice

A jockey who is in training. "Also note that a horse that runs today at, say, 115 pounds without an *apprentice* allowance, and who ran last time at 115 with an apprentice allowance is actually taking a five-pound weight drop."

Backed

Refers to a horse that has been heavily bet on. "The horse that wins is usually well *backed*, as evidenced by the odds."

Breezing

A horse that is running at moderate speed. "A convincing winner is one that wins easily, handily, *breezing* or even driving when he outdistances his competition by a length or more."

Bug

A jockey with an apprentice standing. "The fact that a promising jockey often fades when he loses the bug is nothing against the young man."

Claiming Race (Claimer)

A race in which each horse can be purchased at a predetermined price. "When the race is a *claimer* for four-year-olds or older, a gelding has an edge over his running mates."

Class

A horse's rank or potential, as indicated by his previous record. "The higher the average earnings, the greater the horse's potential or *class*."

Colt

A male horse, four-years-old or younger, that has not been gelded. "Failure to force *colts* to the limit may end in defeat."

Daily Racing Form

A daily newspaper that gives racing news and past performance data on horses, including handicapping. "The *Daily Racing Form* contains everything that is essential to the bettor taking a calculated risk."

Distance

The length of a race. "The most common short race is six furlongs in *distance*."

Driving

The jockey strongly urges the horse to run faster. "We would like to see the way in which the winners and other good performers finished; for example, whether the horse won *driving*, handily, or so on."

Fast Track

A dirt track in optimum condition: dry, even, and resilient. "It is well known that certain horses do relatively better in the mud than they do on a *fast track*."

GLOSSARY

Favorite
> The horse that is quoted at the lowest odds. "Even the *favorite* will win three to four races out of ten, despite the fact that he often becomes the *favorite* by excess betting on the part of people who depend on dope sheets."

Field
> All the horses that are running in a race. "Off-days cannot be explained by the *field* that is running."

Filly
> A female horse that is four-years-old or younger. "The abbreviation for *filly* is "**f.**""

Form
> The performance records of a horse and his expected current performance. "In some of these cases, the horses are unreliable or have not yet developed a *form* (two-year-olds, maidens, cheap or old steeds)." Also, an abbreviation for the *Daily Racing Form*.

Front Runner
> A horse that usually tries to get the lead at the start of the race and stay there for as long as he can. "In the short races, a fast breaker and *front runner* in an inside post position does seem to have the advantage."

Furlong
> One-eighth of a mile. "The most common short race is six *furlongs*, and is also the best short distance for betting purposes."

Gelding
> A male horse that has been castrated. "When the race is a claimer for four-year-olds or older, a *gelding* has an edge over his running mates."

Handicap Race
> A race in which the track's handicapper assigns the weights to be carried on the assumption that horses will then run on a fair and equal basis. "The most significant drops are those from *handicaps* to allowances, or from either of these to claimers."

Handicapping

Selecting a steed to bet on, based on its past performance. "There are several approaches to *handicapping* that will give three wins in ten selections."

Heavy Track

The wettest possible condition of the turf. "In short races, add 3 points for good, 8 for slow, 10 for sloppy, 15 for mud, and 20 for *heavy tracks*."

Horse

In common usage, "horse" means an equine. In horseracing, when referring to an entrant's sex, "horse" means a five-year-old male that has not been gelded. "The abbreviation used to denote a *horse's* sex and age is "**h**."

Length

Approximately eight feet, which is about the length of a horse from nose to tail. "Give one point to the mounts that won or were within two *lengths* of the winner in the last race."

Long Odds

More than 10 to 1. "When a horse is listed at *long odds* in the morning line and they fall noticeably at the track—say from 15 to 1 to 6 to 1 or less—those who know horses are betting on the steed."

Longshot

A horse that appears to have only a slim chance of winning, and will return high odds if he does. "A rather common bettor's malady is consistent *longshot* betting, with or without recommending qualities in the selection."

Maiden

A horse that has not won a race. "Skip *maidens* and mounts just off a *maiden* win."

Maiden Race

A race in which none of the horses has a previous win. "It is probably all right to bet on a mount off a *maiden* win if the race in which he broke his maiden status was at a speed rating lower than he had earned in a previous race."

Mare

A female horse that is five-years-old or older. "It is probable that a gelding with average winnings of $300 per race is a match for a *mare* or horse averaging $450 to $500."

Meet

A collection of races conducted by a club on its track. "Tracks differ, and the more often a horse runs in a *meet*, the better for him."

Morning Line

The odds quoted before wagering begins. "When a horse is listed at long odds in the *morning line* and they fall noticeably at the track—say from 15 to 1 to 6 to 1 or less—those who know horses are betting on the steed."

Muddy Track

A racetrack that is wet but has no standing water. "Some handicappers consider the low weight a definite advantage when the track is *muddy*."

Odds

The chances of a horse winning, from a sportsbook or bookmaker's point of view, adjusted to include a profit. "In fact, the longer the *odds*, the less often does the horse come in."

Pari-mutuel

A form of wagering in which all the money that has been bet is divided among those bettors who have winning tickets—after taxes, takeout and other deductions are made. "*Pari-mutuel* betting need be no more a case of gambling than is investing in stocks or bonds or any business venture."

Place

Finish second. "It is easier to forecast the winner than the horse that will *place* or show."

Post

The starting point for a race. "Say a horse quoted at 3 to 1 in the morning is going to *post* at 5 to 1. You may have a good bet."

Post Position

The position of the stall in the starting gate that a horse starts from in the race. "One element in a race is pure chance—the horse's *post position*, which is chosen by lot."

Purse

The prize money. "Skip the great classics where the *purse* is exceptionally high."

Rating

A horse's rating reflects his chance of winning a race, as determined by handicappers or tip sheets. "The mount with the highest *rating* (not counting the last race) during the last sixty days deserves a point and so does the entrant with the best backlog of *ratings*."

Ridgling

A male horse with one or both testicles undescended. "The common abbreviation used to denote a *ridgling* is "**r.**""

Scratch

Removed from a race before it starts, often because of bad track condition or the horse's health. "By making your selections after *scratches* have been made, you will avoid wasting your time on mounts that may not even run."

Show

Third position at the finish. "For mounts going to post at 10 to 1 or better, bet win and *show*."

Show Bet

A wager that a horse will finish in the money; that is, third or better. "It is better to collect *show* money than no money!"

Short Race

A race that is under a mile. "Some of the points that are against a horse in a *short race* may be in his favor in a long one and vice versa."

Sloppy Track

A track that is wet on the surface, but firm underneath. "In short races, add 3 points for good, 8 for slow, 10 for *sloppy tracks* …"

Slow Track
> A track that is wet on both the surface and base. "In short races, add 3 points for good, 8 for *slow tracks* ..."

Stretch
> The last straight portion of the racetrack to the finish line. "Bet to win in long races when the mount was first at the *stretch* call last race."

Ticket
> The betting slip or ticket that a bettor receives as proof of his wager, and which must be shown to collect any winnings. "In other words, when we do collect, we must average $6.70 or better for $2.00 *tickets*."

Track Condition
> The condition of the racetrack's surface, such as fast, slow or muddy. "Judge turf and other off track entrants by the records they made at today's distance and *track condition*."

Trainer
> The licensed person who cares for and prepares a horse to race. "Often, your judgment will be better than that of the *trainer*. After all, trainers are often prejudiced."

Turf (course)
> A grass course. "It is probable that *turf* and mud races could be forecast if there were more of them."

Wire
> The finish line of a race. "It is sufficient for back runners that they got to the *wire*."

ATTENTION: HORSE BETTORS!

If you like this book, come to our website, and browse our extensive library of titles—we not only have the world's largest selection of horseracing titles (*more than 20 times* the selection of chain superstores), but over 3,000 total gaming and gambling titles!